MENTAL

Two Booklets

. . .

ON UNION
WITH
GOD
BY SAINT ALBERT THE GREAT, O.P.

And

AN EASY METHOD
OF
MENTAL PRAYER
BY FR. BERTRAND WILBERFORCE, O.P.

Published by Lunae Lumen Libris © 2022
All rights reserved.
ISBN: 9798805485252

Contents

ON UNION WITH GOD
BY SAINT ALBERT THE GREAT, O.P.

WITH NOTES BY REV. P. J. BERTHIER, O.P.

TRANSLATED BY A BENEDICTINE OF PRINCETHORPE PRIORY

Nihil Obstat.
F. THOS. BERGH, O.S.B.,
CENSOR DEPUTATUS.

Imprimatur.
EDM. CAN. SURMONT,
VICARIUS GENERALIS.

WESTMONASTERII,
Die 7 Decembris, 1911.

Preface

Surely the most deeply-rooted need of the human soul, its purest aspiration, is for the closest possible union with God. As one turns over the pages of this little work, written by Saint Albert the Great[1] towards the end of his life, when that great soul had ripened and matured, one feels that here indeed is the ideal of one's hopes.

Simply and clearly the great principles are laid down, the way is made plain which leads to the highest spiritual life. It seems as though, while one reads, the mists of earth vanish, and the snowy summits appear of the mountains of God. We breathe only the pure atmosphere of prayer, peace, and love, and the one great fact of the universe, the Divine Presence, is felt and realized without effort.

But is such a life possible amid the whirl of the twentieth century? To faith and love all things are possible, and our author shows us the loving Father, ever ready to give as much and more than we can ask. The spirit of such a work is ever true; the application may vary with circumstances, but the guidance of the Holy Spirit will never be

---

[1] Following the general tradition, we attribute this work to Albert the Great, but not all critics are agreed as to its authenticity.

wanting to those souls who crave for closer union with their Divine Master.

This little treatise has been very aptly called the "Metaphysics of the Imitation," and it is in the hope that it may be of use to souls that it has been translated into English.

Saint Albert the Great is too well known for it to be necessary for us to give more than the briefest outline of his life.

The eldest son of the Count of Bollstädt, he was born at Lauingen in Swabia in 1205 or 1206, though some historians give it as 1193. As a youth he was sent to the University of Padua, where he had special facilities for the study of the liberal arts.

Drawn by the persuasive teaching of Blessed Jordan of Saxony, he joined the Order of St. Dominic in 1223, and after completing his studies, received the Doctor's degree at the University of Paris.

His brilliant genius quickly brought him into the most prominent positions. Far-famed for his learning, he attracted scholars from all parts of Europe to Paris, Cologne, Ratisbon, etc., where he successively taught. It was during his years of teaching at Paris and Cologne that he counted among his disciples St. Thomas Aquinas, the greatness of whose future he foretold, and whose lifelong friendship with him then began.

In 1254 Albert was elected Provincial of his Order in Germany. In 1260 he was appointed Bishop of Ratisbon, but resigned his see in 1262. He then continued unweariedly until a few years before his death, when his great powers, especially his memory, failed him, but the fervor of his soul remained ever the same. In 1280, at Cologne, he sank, at last worn out by his manifold labors.

"Whether we consider him as a theologian or as a philosopher, Albert was undoubtedly one of the most extraordinary men of his age; I might say, one of the most wonderful men of genius who appeared in past times" (Jourdain).

Very grateful thanks are due to Rev. P. J. Berthier, O.P., for his kind permission to append to this edition a translation of his excellent notes (from the French edition, entitled "De l'Union avec Dieu").

Publishers Note

Blessed Albert the Great and *Blessed* Isaac have been canonized since the original publication, and their titles have been updated to *Saint*.

Chapter I – Of The Highest Perfection Which Man Can Attain Unto In This Life

I have felt moved to write a few last thoughts describing, as far as one may in this waiting-time of our exile and pilgrimage, the entire separation of the soul from all earthly things and its close, unfettered union with God.

I have been the more urged to this, because Christian perfection has no other end but charity, which unites us to God.[2]

This union of charity is essential for salvation, since it consists in the practice of the precepts and in conformity to the Divine will. Hence it separates us from whatever would war against the essence and habit of charity, such as mortal sin.[3]

But religious, the more easily to attain to God, their last end, have gone beyond this, and have bound themselves by vow to evangelical perfection, to that which is voluntary and of counsel.[4] With the help of these vows they cut off

---

[2] Albert the Great is speaking here in a special manner of religious perfection, although what he says is also true of Christian perfection in general.

[3] He speaks here of the obligation laid upon all Christians.

[4] Religious bind themselves to observe as a duty that which was only of counsel. To them, therefore, the practice of the counsels becomes an obligation.

all that might impede the fervor of their love or hinder them in their flight to God. They have, therefore, by the vow of their religious profession, renounced all things, whether pertaining to soul or body.[5] God is in truth a Spirit, and "they that adore Him must adore Him in spirit and in truth,"[6] that is, with a knowledge and love, an intelligence and will purified from every phantom of earth.

Hence it is written: "When thou shalt pray, enter into thy chamber"--i.e., into the inmost abode of thy heart--and, "having shut the door" of thy senses, with a pure heart, a free conscience and an unfeigned faith, "pray to thy Father" in spirit and in truth, in the "secret" of thy soul.[7]

Then only will a man attain to this ideal, when he has despoiled and stripped himself of all else; when, wholly recollected within himself, he has hidden from and forgotten the whole world, that he may abide in silence in the presence of Jesus Christ. There, in solitude of soul, with loving confidence he makes known his desires to God. With all the

---

[5] The vows of religious have as their immediate object the removal of obstacles to perfection, but they do not in themselves constitute perfection. Perfection consists in charity. Albert the Great speaks of only one vow, because in his day the formulas of religious profession mentioned only the vow of obedience, which includes the other two vows.

[6] John iv. 24.

[7] Matt. vi. 6.

intensity of his love he pours forth his heart before Him, in sincerity and truth, until he loses himself in God. Then is his heart enlarged, inflamed, and melted in him, yea, even in its inmost depths.

Chapter II – How A Man May Despise All Things And Cleave To Christ Alone

Whosoever thou art who longest to enter upon this happy state or seekest to direct thither thy steps, thus it behoveth thee to act.

First, close, as it were, thine eyes, and bar the doors of thy senses. Suffer not anything to entangle thy soul, nor permit any care or trouble to penetrate within it.

Shake off all earthly things, counting them useless, noxious, and hurtful to thee.[8]

When thou hast done this, enter wholly within thyself, and fix thy gaze upon thy wounded Jesus, and upon Him alone. Strive with all thy powers, unwearyingly, to reach God through Himself, that is, through God made Man, that thou mayest attain to the knowledge of His Divinity through the wounds of His Sacred Humanity.

In all simplicity and confidence abandon thyself and whatever concerns thee without reserve to

---

[8] When Albert the Great and the other mystics warn us against solicitude with regard to creatures, they refer to that solicitude which is felt for creatures in themselves; they do not mean that we ought not to occupy ourselves with them in any way for God's sake. The great doctor explains his meaning in clear terms later on in this work.

God's unfailing Providence, according to the teaching of St. Peter: "Casting all your care upon Him,"[9] Who can do all things. And again, it is written: "Be nothing solicitous";[10] "Cast thy care upon the Lord and He shall sustain thee";[11] "It is good for me to adhere to my God";[12] "I set the Lord always in my sight";[13] "I found Him Whom my soul loveth";[14] and "Now all good things came to me"[15] together with Him. This is the hidden and heavenly treasure, the precious pearl, which is to be preferred before all. This it is that we must seek with humble confidence and untiring effort, yet in silence and peace.

It must be sought with a brave heart, even though its price be the loss of bodily comfort, of esteem, and of honour.

Lacking this, what doth it profit a religious if he "gain the whole world, and suffer the loss of his own soul?"[16]. Of what value are the religious state, the holiness of our profession, the shaven head, the outward signs of a life of abnegation, if we lack the

_____

[9] 1 Pet. v. 7.
[10] Phil. iv. 6
[11] Ps. liv. 23.
[12] Ps. lxxii. 28.
[13] Ps. xv. 8.
[14] Cant. iii. 4.
[15] Wis. vii. 11.
[16] Matt. xvi. 26.

spirit of humility and truth, in which Christ dwells by faith and love? St. Luke says: "The kingdom of God," that is, Christ, "is within you."[17]

---

[17] Luke xvii. 21

Chapter III – The Law Of Man's Perfection In This Life

In proportion as the mind is absorbed in the thought and care of the things of this world do we lose the fervor of our devotion, and drift away from the things of Heaven.

The greater, on the other hand, our diligence in withdrawing our powers from the memory, love and thought of that which is inferior in order to fix them upon that which is above, the more perfect will be our prayer, the purer our contemplation. The soul cannot give itself perfectly at the same time to two objects as contrary one to another as light to darkness;[18] for he who lives united to God dwells in the light, he who clings to this world lives in darkness.

The highest perfection, therefore, of man in this life lies in this: that he is so united to God that his soul with all its powers and faculties becomes recollected in Him and is one spirit with Him.[19] Then it remembers naught save God, nor does it

---

[18] Albert the Great supposes here that we give ourselves equally to God and to creatures, which would be wrong, and not that creatures are subordinated to God, which would be a virtue.
[19] This must be understood to mean that God is the principal and supreme end of all created activities.

relish or understand anything but Him. Then all its affections, united in the delights of love, repose sweetly in the enjoyment of their Creator.

The image of God which is imprinted upon the soul is found in the three powers of the reason, memory, and will. But since these do not perfectly bear the Divine likeness, they have not the same resemblance to God as in the first days of man's creation.[20]

God is the "form" of the soul upon which He must impress His own image, as the seal on the wax or the stamp on the object it marks.[21]

This can only be fully accomplished when the reason is wholly illuminated according to its capacity, by the knowledge of God, the Sovereign Truth; the will entirely devoted to the love of the Supreme Good; the memory absorbed in the

---

[20] The perfect image of God in man does not consist merely in the possession of those faculties by which we resemble Him, but rather in performing by faith and love, as far as is in our power, acts like those which He performs, in knowing Him as He knows Himself, in loving Him as He loves Himself.

[21] In scholastic theology the term "form" is used of that which gives to anything its accidental or substantial being. God is the "accidental form" of the soul, because in giving it its activity He bestows upon it something of His own activity, by means of sanctifying grace. Yet more truly may it be said that God is also the "form" of the soul in the sense that it is destined by the ordinary workings of Providence to participate by sanctifying grace in the Being of God, enjoying thus a participation real, though created, in the Divine nature.

contemplation and enjoyment of eternal felicity, and in the sweet repose of so great a happiness.

As the perfect possession of this state constitutes the glory of the Blessed in Heaven, it is clear that in its commencement consists the perfection of this life.

Chapter IV – That Our Labor Must Be With The Understanding And Not With The Senses

Blessed is he who by continually cleansing his soul from the images and phantoms of earth draws its powers inward, and thence lifts them up to God.

At length he in a manner forgets all images, and by a simple and direct act of pure intellect and will contemplates God, Who is absolutely simple.

Cast from thee, therefore, all phantoms, images, and forms, and whatsoever is not God,[22] that all thy intercourse with Him may proceed from an understanding, affection, and will, alike purified. This is, in truth, the end of all thy labors, that thou mayest draw nigh unto God and repose in Him within thy soul, solely by thy understanding and by a fervent love, free from entanglement or earthly image.

Not by his bodily organs or outward senses does a man attain to this, but by the intelligence and will, which constitute him man.[23] So long as he lingers,

---

[22] We must avoid these things in so far as they separate us from God, but they may also serve to draw us nearer to Him if we regard them in God and for God.

[23] It is by the intelligence and will that man actually attains to this, but the use of the sensitive faculties is presupposed.

trifling with the objects of the imagination and senses, he has not yet passed beyond the limits and instincts of his animal nature, which he possesses in common with the brute beasts. They know and feel through images and by their senses, nor can it be otherwise, for they have no higher powers. Not so is it with man, who, by his intelligence, affections, and will, is created in the image and likeness of God. Hence it is by these powers that he ought, without intermediary, purely and directly to commune with God, be united to Him, and cleave to Him.[24]

The Devil does his very utmost to hinder us from this exercise, for he beholds in it a beginning and a foretaste of eternal life, and he is envious of man. Therefore, he strives, now by one temptation or passion, now by another, to turn away our thoughts from God.

At one time he assails us by arousing in us unnecessary anxiety, foolish cares or troubles, or by drawing us to irregular conversations and vain curiosity. At another he ensnares us by subtle books, by the words of others, by rumors and novelties. Then, again, he has recourse to trials, contradictions, etc.

---

[24] The sensitive faculties, if used as a means, often help us to draw near to God, but when used as an end, their activity becomes an obstacle

Although these things may sometimes seem but very trifling faults, if faults at all, yet do they greatly hinder our progress in this holy exercise. Therefore, whether great or small, they must be resisted and driven from us as evil and harmful, though they may seem useful and even necessary. It is of great importance that what we have heard, or seen, or done, or said, should not leave their traces or fill our imagination.

Neither before nor after, nor at the time, should we foster these memories or allow their images to be formed. For when the mind is free from these thoughts, we are not hindered in our prayer, in meditation, or the psalmody, or in any other of our spiritual exercises, nor do these distractions return to trouble us.

Then should thou readily and trustfully commit thyself and all that concerns thee to the unfailing and most sure Providence of God, in silence and peace. He Himself will fight for thee, and will grant thee a liberty and consolation better, nobler, and sweeter than would be possible if thou gave thyself up day and night to thy fancies, to vain and wandering thoughts, which hold captive the mind, as they toss it hither and thither, wearying soul and body, and wasting uselessly alike thy time and strength.[25]

Accept all things, whatsoever their cause, silently and with a tranquil mind, as coming to thee from the fatherly hand of Divine Providence.

Free thyself, therefore, from all the impressions of earthly things, in so far as thy state and profession require, so that with a purified mind and sincere affection thou mayest cleave to Him to Whom thou hast so often and so entirely vowed thyself.

Let nothing remain which could come between thy soul and God, that so thou mayest be able to pass surely and directly from the wounds of the Sacred Humanity to the brightness of the Divinity.

---

[25]This teaching is the Christian rendering of the axiom formulated by the Philosopher: "Homo sedendo fit sapiens"--"It is in quiet that man gains wisdom."

Chapter V – Of Purity Of Heart, Which Is To Be Sought Above All Else

Wouldst thou journey by the shortest road, the straight and safe way unto eternal bliss, unto thy true country, to grace and glory? Strive with all thy might to obtain habitual cleanness of heart, purity of mind, quiet of the senses. Gather up thy affections, and with thy whole heart cleave unto God.

Withdraw as much as thou canst from thy acquaintance and from all men, and abstain from such affairs as would hinder thy purpose.

Seek out with jealous care the place, time, and means most suited to quiet and contemplation, and lovingly embrace silence and solitude.

Beware the dangers of which the times are full; fly the agitation of a world never at rest, never still.[26]

Let thy chief study be to gain purity, freedom, and peace of heart. Close the doors of thy senses and dwell within, shutting thy heart as diligently as thou canst against the shapes and images of earthly things.

---

[26] This is especially true for religious.

Of all the practices of the spiritual life purity of heart stands highest, and rightly, for it is the end and reward of all our labors, and is found only with those who live truly according to the spirit and as good religious.

Wherefore thou shouldst employ all thy diligence and skill in order to free thy heart, senses, and affections from whatever could trammel their liberty, or could fetter or ensnare thy soul. Strive earnestly to gather in the wandering affections of thy heart and fix them on the love of the sole and pure Truth, the Sovereign Good; then keep them, as it were, enchained within thee.

Fix thy gaze unwaveringly upon God and Divine things; spurn the follies of earth and seek to be wholly transformed in Jesus Christ, yea, even to the heart's core.

When thou hast begun to cleanse and purify thy soul of earthly images, and to unify and tranquillize thy heart and mind in God with loving confidence, to the end that thou mayest taste and enjoy in all thy powers the torrents of His good pleasure, and mayest fix thy will and intelligence in Him, then thou wilt no longer need to study and read the Holy Scriptures to learn the love of God and of thy neighbour, for the Holy Spirit Himself will teach thee.[27]

Spare no pains, no labour, to purify thy heart and to establish it in unbroken peace.

Abide in God in the secret place of thy soul as tranquilly as though there had already risen upon thee the dawn of Eternity, the unending Day of God.

Strong in the love of Jesus, go forth from thyself, with a heart pure, a conscience at peace, a faith unfeigned; and in every trial, every event, commit thyself unreservedly to God, having nothing so much at heart as perfect obedience to His will and good pleasure.

If thou wouldst arrive thus far, it is needful for thee often to enter within thy soul and to abide therein, disengaging thyself as much as thou canst from all things.

Keep the eye of thy soul ever in purity and peace; suffer not the form and images of this world to defile thy mind; preserve thy will from every earthly care, and let every fibre of thy heart be rooted in the love of the Sovereign Good. Thus will

---

[27] By this is meant that the Holy Scriptures, though always presupposed as the foundation of our belief, of themselves give only an objective knowledge of God, while that which the Holy Ghost gives is experimental.

thy whole soul, with all its powers, be recollected in God and form but one spirit with Him.

It is in this that the highest perfection possible to man here below consists.

This union of the spirit and of love, by which a man conforms himself in everything to the supreme and eternal will, enables us to become by grace what God is by His nature.[28]

Let us not forget this truth: the moment a man, by the help of God, succeeds in overcoming his own will, that is, in freeing himself from every inordinate affection and care, to cast himself and all his miseries unreservedly into the bosom of God, that moment he becomes so pleasing to God that he receives the gift of grace. Grace brings charity, and charity drives out all fear and hesitation, and fills the soul with confidence and hope. What is more blessed than to cast all our care on Him Who cannot fail? As long as thou leanest upon thyself thou wilt totter. Cast thyself fearlessly into the arms of God. He will embrace thee, He will heal and save thee.[29]

---

[28] God knows and loves Himself in Himself by His own nature, while we know and love Him in Himself by grace.

[29] A very striking feature in the doctrine of this book is that it requires first the perfection of the soul and the faculties, whence proceeds that of our actions. Some modern authors, confining themselves to casuistry, speak almost exclusively of the perfection of actions, a method less logical and less thorough.

If thou wouldst ponder often upon these truths they would bring to thee more happiness than all the riches, delights, honours, of this false world, and would make thee more blessed than all the wisdom and knowledge of this corruptible life, even though thou shouldst surpass all the wise men who have gone before thee.

Chapter VI – That A Man Truly Devout Must Seek God In Purity Of Mind And Heart

As thou goest forward in this work of ridding thee of every earthly thought and entanglement thou wilt behold thy soul regain her strength and the mastery of her inward senses, and thou wilt begin to taste the sweetness of heavenly things.

Learn, therefore, to keep thyself free from the images of outward and material objects, for God loves with a special love the soul that is thus purified. His "delights" are "to be with the children of men,"[30] that is, with those who, set free from earthly affairs and distractions, and at peace from their passions, offer Him simple and pure hearts intent on Him alone.

If the memory, imagination, and thoughts still dwell below, it follows of necessity that fresh events, memories of the past, and other things will ensnare and drag thee down. But the Holy Spirit abides not amid such empty thoughts.

The true friend of Jesus Christ must be so united by his intelligence and will to the Divine will and

---

[30] Prov. viii. 31.

goodness that his imagination and passions have no hold over him, and that he troubles not whether men give him love or ridicule, nor heeds what may be done to him. Know well that a truly good will does all and is of more value than all.

If the will is good, wholly conformed and united to God, and guided by reason, it matters little that the flesh, the senses, the exterior man are inclined to evil and sluggish in good, or even that a man find himself interiorly lacking in devotion.[31] It suffices that he remains with his whole soul inwardly united to God by faith and a good will.

This he will accomplish if, knowing his own imperfection and utter nothingness, he understands that all his happiness is in his Creator. Then does he forsake himself, his own strength and powers, and every creature, and hides himself in complete abandonment in the bosom of God.

To God are all his actions simply and purely directed. He seeks nothing outside of God, but knows that of a truth he has found in Him all the good and all the happiness of perfection. Then will he be in some measure transformed in God. He will no longer be able to think, love, understand, remember aught save God and the things of God. He

---

[31] The exterior powers of a man are the imagination and passions; the interior his intelligence and will, which sometimes find themselves deprived of all the aids of sensible devotion.

will no longer behold himself or creatures save in God; no love will possess him but the love of God, nor will he remember creatures or even his own being, save in God.

Such a knowledge of the truth renders the soul humble, makes her a hard judge towards herself, but merciful to others, while earthly wisdom puffs up the soul with pride and vanity. Behold, this is wise and spiritual doctrine, grounded upon the truth, and leading unto the knowledge and service of God, and to familiarity with Him.

If thou desirest to possess Him indeed, thou must of necessity despoil thy heart of earthly affections, not alone for persons, but for every creature, that thou mayest tend to the Lord thy God with thy whole heart and with all thy strength, freely, simply, without fear or solicitude, trusting everything in entire confidence to His all-watchful Providence.[32]

---

[32] In truth, all the designs of God in our regard are full of mercy, and tend especially to our sanctification; the obstacles to these designs come only from our evil passions.

Chapter VII – On The Practice Of Interior Recollection

The author of the book entitled "De Spiritu et Anima" tells us (chap. xxi.)[33] that to ascend to God means nothing else than to enter into oneself. And, indeed, he who enters into the secret place of his own soul passes beyond himself, and does in very truth ascend to God.

Banish, therefore, from thy heart the distractions of earth and turn thine eyes to spiritual joys, that thou mayest learn at last to repose in the light of the contemplation of God.

Verily the soul's true life and her repose are to abide in God, held fast by love, and sweetly refreshed by the Divine consolations.

But many are the obstacles which hinder us from tasting this rest, and of our own strength we could never attain to it. The reason is evident--the mind is distracted and preoccupied; it cannot enter into itself by the aid of the memory, for it is blinded by phantoms; nor can it enter by the intellect, for it is vitiated by the passions. Even the desire of interior joys and spiritual delights fails to draw it inward. It

---

[33] The book "De Spiritu et Anima" is of uncertain authorship. It is printed after the works of St. Augustine in Migne's "Patrologia Latina," vol. xl., 779.

lies so deeply buried in things sensible and transitory that it cannot return to itself as to the image of God.

How needful is it, then, that the soul, lifted upon the wings of reverence and humble confidence, should rise above itself and every creature by entire detachment, and should be able to say within itself: He Whom I seek, love, desire, among all, more than all, and above all, cannot be perceived by the senses or the imagination, for He is above both the senses and the understanding. He cannot be perceived by the senses, yet He is the object of all our desires; He is without shape, but He is supremely worthy of our heart's deepest love. He is beyond compare, and to the pure in heart greatly to be desired. Above all else is He sweet and love-worthy; His goodness and perfection are infinite.

When thou shalt understand this, thy soul will enter into the darkness of the spirit, and will advance further and penetrate more deeply into itself.[34] Thou wilt by this means attain more

---

[34] This darkness is the silence of the imagination, which no longer gains a hearing, and that of the intellect, which is sufficiently enlightened to understand that we can in reality understand nothing of the Divinity in itself, and that the best thing we can do is to remove from our conception of God all those limitations which we observe in creatures. The reason of this is that we can only know God naturally by means of what we see in creatures, and these are always utterly insufficient to give us an adequate idea of the Creator.

speedily unto the beholding in a dark manner of the Trinity in Unity, and Unity in Trinity, in Christ Jesus, in proportion as thy effort is more inward; and the greater is thy charity, the more precious the fruit thou wilt reap. For the highest, in spiritual things, is ever that which is most interior. Grow not weary, therefore, and rest not from thy efforts until thou hast received some earnest or foretaste of the fulness of joy that awaits thee and has obtained some first-fruits of the Divine sweetness and delights.

Cease not in thy pursuit till thou shalt behold "the God of gods in Sion."[35]

In thy spiritual ascent and in thy search after a closer union with God thou must allow thyself no repose, no slipping back, but must go forward till thou hast obtained the object of thy desires. Follow the example of mountain-climbers. If thy desires turn aside after the objects which pass below thou wilt lose thyself in byways and countless distractions. Thy mind will become dissipated and drawn in all directions by its desires. Thy progress will be uncertain, thou wilt not reach thy goal, nor find rest after thy labors.

If, on the other hand, the heart and mind, led on by love and desire, withdraw from the distractions

---

[35] Ps. lxxxiii. 8.

of this world, and little by little abandon baser things to become recollected in the one true and unchangeable Good, to dwell there, held fast by the bonds of love, then wilt thou grow strong, and thy recollection will deepen the higher thou risest on the wings of knowledge and desire.

They who have attained to this dwell as by habit in the Sovereign Good, and become at last inseparable from it.

True life, which is God Himself, becomes their inalienable possession;[36] forever, free from all fear of the vicissitudes of time and change[37] (see footnote), they repose in the peaceful enjoyment of this inward happiness, and in sweet communication with God. Their abode is for ever fixed within their own souls, in Christ Jesus, Who is to all who come to Him "the Way, the Truth, and the Life."[38]

---

[36] We only lose God, the uncreated Good, by an unlawful attachment to created good; if we are free from this attachment, we tend to Him without effort.

[37] The subsequent condemnation, in 1687, of this doctrine, as taught by Molino, could not, of course, be foreseen by Saint Albertus writing in the thirteenth century.

[38] John xiv. 6

Chapter VIII – That A Truly Devout Man Should Commit Himself To God In All That Befalls Him

From all that has hitherto been said, thou hast understood, if I mistake not, that the more thou separatest thyself from earthly images and created objects, and the closer thy union with God, the nearer wilt thou approach to the state of innocence and perfection. What could be happier, better, sweeter than this?

It is, therefore, of supreme importance that thou shouldst preserve thy soul so free from every trace or entanglement of earth that neither the world nor thy friends, neither prosperity nor adversity, things present, past, or future, which concern thyself or others, not even thine own sins above measure, should have power to trouble thee.

Think only how thou mayest live, as it were, alone with God, removed from the world, the simple and pure life of the spirit, as though thy soul were already in eternity and separated from thy body.

There thou wouldst not busy thyself with earthly things, nor be disquieted by the state of the world, by peace or war, fair skies or foul, or anything here below. But thou wouldst be absorbed and filled by His love.

Strive even now in this present life to come forth in a manner from thy body and from every creature.

As far as thou canst, fix the eye of thy soul steadfastly, with unobscured gaze, upon the uncreated light.

Then will thy soul, purified from the clouds of earth, be like an Angel in a human body, no longer troubled by the flesh, or disturbed by vain thoughts.

Arm thyself against temptations, persecutions, injuries, so that in adversity as in prosperity, thou mayest still cleave to God in unbroken peace.

When trouble, discouragement, confusion of mind assail thee, do not lose patience or be cast down. Do not betake thee to vocal prayers or other consolations, but endeavour by an act of the will and reason to lift up thy soul and unite it to God, whether thy sensual nature will or no.

The devout soul should be so united to God, should so form and preserve her will in conformity to the Divine will, that she is no more occupied or allured by any creature than before it was created, but lives as though there existed but God and herself.[39]

She will receive in unvarying peace all that comes to her from the hand of Divine Providence. In all things she will hope in the Lord, without losing patience, peace, or silence.

Behold, therefore, of how great value it is in the spiritual life to be detached from all things, that thou mayest be interiorly united to God and conformed to Him. Moreover, there will then be no longer anything to intervene between thy soul and God. Whence could it come? Not from without, for the vow of voluntary poverty has despoiled thee of all earthly goods, that of chastity has taken thy body. Nor could it come from within, for obedience has taken from thee thy very will and soul. There is now nothing left which could come between God and thyself.

That thou art a religious, thy profession, thy state, thy habit and tonsure, and the other marks of the religious life declare. See to it whether thou art a religious in truth or only one in name.

Consider how thou art fallen and how thou sinnest against the Lord thy God and against His justice if thy deeds do not correspond with thy holy

---

[39] And this she does because creatures no longer occupy her, except for God's sake.

state, if by will or desire thou clingest to the creature rather than to the Creator, or preferrest the creature to the Creator.

Chapter IX – The Contemplation Of God Is To Be Preferred Above All Other Exercises

Whatever exists outside of God is the work of His hands. Every creature is, therefore, a blending together of the actual and the possible, and as such is in its nature limited. Born of nothing, it is surrounded by nothingness, and tends to nothingness.[40]

Of necessity the creature depends each moment upon God, the supreme Artist, for its existence, preservation, power of action, and all that it possesses.

It is utterly unable to accomplish its own work, either for itself or for another, and is impotent as a thing which is not before that which is, the finite before the infinite. It follows, therefore, that our life, thoughts, and works should be in Him, of Him, for Him, and directed to Him, Who by the least sign of His will could produce creatures unspeakably more perfect than any which now exist.

It is impossible that there should be in the mind or heart a thought or a love more profitable, more perfect or more blessed than those which rest upon

---

[40] This is so because, according to true philosophy, the essence of a thing is distinct from its existence.

God, the Almighty Creator, of Whom, in Whom, by Whom, towards Whom all tend.

He suffices infinitely for Himself and for others, since from all eternity He contains within Himself the perfections of all things. There is nothing within Him which is not Himself. In Him and by Him exist the causes of all transitory things; in Him are the immutable origins of all things that change, whether rational or irrational.

All that happens in time has in Him its eternal principle.

He fills all; He is in all things by His essence, by which He is more present and more near to them than they are to themselves.[41]

In Him all things are united and live eternally.[42] It is true that the weakness of our understanding or our want of experience[43] may oblige us to make use of creatures in our contemplation, yet there is a kind of contemplation which is very fruitful, good, and real, which seems possible to all. Whether he meditates on the creature or the Creator, every man may reach the point at which he finds all his joy in

---

[41] Every actual cause is more intimately present to its accomplished work than the work itself, which it necessarily precedes.

[42] John i. 3, 4.

[43] We cannot always experience Divine things, and at first we can only compare them to the things which we experience here below.

His Creator, God, One in Trinity, and kindles the fire of Divine love in himself or in others, so as to merit eternal life.

We should notice here the difference which exists between the contemplation of Christians and that of pagan philosophers. The latter sought only their own perfection, and hence their contemplation affected their intellect only; they desired only to enrich their minds with knowledge. But the contemplation of Saints, which is that of Christians, seeks as its end the love of the God Whom they contemplate. Hence it is not content to find fruit for the intelligence, but penetrates beyond to the will that it may there enkindle love.

The Saints desired above all in their contemplation the increase of charity.

It is better to know Jesus Christ and possess Him spiritually by grace, than, without grace, to have Him in the body, or even in His essence.

The more pure a soul becomes and the deeper her recollection, the clearer will be her inward vision. She now prepares, as it were, a ladder upon which she may ascend to the contemplation of God. This contemplation will set her on fire with love for all that is heavenly, Divine, eternal, and will cause her to despise as utter nothing all that is of time.

When we seek to arrive at the knowledge of God by the method of negation, we first remove from our conception of Him all that pertains to the body, the senses, the imagination. Then we reject even that which belongs to the reason, and the idea of being as it is found in creatures.[44] This, according to St. Denis, is the best means of attaining to the knowledge of God,[45] as far as it is possible in this world.

This is the darkness in which God dwells and into which Moses entered that he might reach the light inaccessible.[46]

But we must begin, not with the mind, but with the body. We must observe the accustomed order, and pass from the labour of action to the repose of contemplation, from the moral virtues to those of sublime contemplation.[47]

---

[44] We deny that there is in God anything which is a mere potentiality, or an imperfection. We deny in Him also the process of reasoning which is the special work of the faculty of reason, because this implies the absence of the vision of truth. We deny "being as it is found in creatures," because in creatures it is necessarily limited, and subject to accident.

45 "Nom. Div.," i.

[46] Exod. xxxiii. 11; Num. xii. 8; Heb. iii. 2.

[47] It would be well to quote St. Thomas, the disciple of Albert the Great, upon this important doctrine: "A thing may be said to belong to the contemplative life in two senses, either as an essential part of it, or as a preliminary disposition. The moral virtues do not belong to the essence of contemplation, whose sole end is the contemplation of truth.... But they belong to it as a necessary predisposition ... because they calm the passions and the tumult of exterior preoccupations, and so facilitate

Why, O my soul, dost thou vainly wear thyself out in such multiplicity of things? Thou findest in them but poverty.

Seek and love only that perfect good which includes in itself all good, and it will suffice thee. Unhappy art thou if thou knowest and possessest all, and art ignorant of this. If thou knewest at the same time both this good and all other things, this alone would render thee the happier. Therefore St. John has written: "This is eternal life: that they may know thee,"[48] and the Prophet: "I shall be satisfied when thy glory shall appear."[49]

---

contemplation" ("Sum.," 2, 2{ae}, q. 180, a. 2). This distinction should never be lost sight of in reading the mystic books of the scholastics.

[48] John xvii. 3.

[49] Ps. xvi. 15

Chapter X – That We Should Not Be Too Solicitous For Actual And Sensible Devotion, But Desire Rather The Union Of Our Will With God

Seek not too eagerly after the grace of devotion, sensible sweetness and tears, but let thy chief care be to remain inwardly united to God by good will in the intellectual part of the soul.[50]

Of a truth nothing is so pleasing to God as a soul freed from all trace and image of created things. A true religious should be at liberty from every creature that he may be wholly free to devote himself to God alone and cleave to Him. Deny thyself, therefore, that thou mayest follow Christ, thy Lord and God, Who was truly poor, obedient, chaste, humble, and suffering, and Whose life and death were a scandal to many, as the Gospel clearly shows.[51]

The soul, when separated from the body, troubles not as to what becomes of the shell it has

---

[50] This admirable doctrine condemns a whole mass of insipid, shallow, affected and sensual books and ideas, which have in modern times flooded the world of piety, have banished from souls more wholesome thoughts, and filled them with a questionable and injurious sentimentality.

[51] Matt. xi. 6; xiii. 57, etc.

abandoned--it may be burnt, hanged, spoken evil of; and the soul is not afflicted by these outrages,[52] but thinks only of eternity and of the one thing necessary, of which the Lord speaks in the Gospel.[53]

So shouldst thou regard thy body, as though the soul were already freed from it. Set ever before thine eyes the eternal life in God, which awaits thee, and think on that only good of which the Lord said: "One thing is necessary."[54] A great grace will then descend upon thy soul, which will aid thee in acquiring purity of mind and simplicity of heart.

And, indeed, this treasure is close at thy doors. Turn from the images and distractions of earth, and quickly shalt thou find it with thee and learn what it is to be united to God without hindrance or impediment.

Then wilt thou gain an unshaken constancy, which will strengthen thee to endure all that may befall thee.

Thus, was it with the martyrs, the Fathers, the elect, and all the blessed. They despised all and thought only of possessing in God eternal security for their souls.

---

[52] This shows an excellent grasp of the meaning of the celebrated maxim "Perinde ac cadaver."
[53] Luke x. 42
[54] *Ibid.*

Thus, armed within and united to God by a good will, they despised all that is of this world, as though their soul had already departed from the body.

Learn from them how great is the power of a good will united to God.

By that union of the soul with God it becomes, as it were, cut off from the flesh by a spiritual separation, and regards the outward man from afar as something alien to it.

Then, whatever may happen inwardly or in the body will be as little regarded as though it had befallen another person or a creature without reason.

He who is united to God is but one mind with Him.

Out of regard, therefore, for His sovereign honour, never be so bold as to think or imagine in His presence what thou wouldst blush to hear or see before men.

Thou oughtest, moreover, to raise all thy thoughts to God alone, and set Him before thine inward gaze, as though He alone existed. So wilt thou experience the sweetness of Divine union and even now make a true beginning of the life to come.

Chapter XI – In What Manner We Should Resist Temptation And Endure Trials

He who with his whole heart draws nigh unto God must of necessity be proved by temptation and trial.

When the sting of temptation is felt, by no means give thy consent, but bear all with patience, sweetness, humility, and courage.

If thou art tempted to blasphemy or any shameful sin, be well assured thou canst do nothing better than to utterly despise and contemn such thoughts. Blasphemy is indeed sinful, scandalous, and abominable, yet be not anxious about such temptations, but rather despise them, and do not let thy conscience be troubled by them. The enemy will most certainly be put to flight if thou wilt thus contemn both him and his suggestions. He is too proud to endure scorn or contempt. The best remedy is, therefore, to trouble no more about these thoughts than we do about the flies which, against our will, dance before our eyes. Let not the servant of Christ thus easily and needlessly lose sight of his Master's presence, nor let him grow impatient, murmur, or complain of these flies; I mean these light temptations, suspicions, sadness, depression, pusillanimity--mere nothings which a good will can put to flight by an elevation of the soul to God.

By a good will man makes God his Master, and the holy Angels his guardians and protectors.

Good will drives away temptation as the hand brushes away a fly.

"Peace," therefore, "to men of good will."[55]

In truth no better gift than this can be offered to God.

Good will in the soul is the source of all good, the mother of all virtues. He who possesses it, possesses without fear of loss all he needs to live a good life.[56]

_____

[55] Luke ii. 14.

[56] Nothing could be more conformable to the teaching of the Gospel than this doctrine.

At His birth Jesus bids the Angels sing that peace belongs to men of good will (Luke ii. 14); later He will declare that His meat is to do the will of His Father (John iv. 34); that He seeks not His own will, but the will of Him Who sent Him (John v. 30); that He came down from heaven to accomplish it (John vi. 38); and when face to face with death He will still pray that the Father's will be done, not His (Matt. xxvi. 39; Luke xxii. 42). Over and over again, in the Gospel, do we find Him using the same language.

He would have His disciples act in the same manner. It is not the man, He tells us, who repeats the words: "My Father, my Father," who shall enter into the Kingdom of Heaven, but he who does the will of God (Matt. vii. 21; Rom. ii. 13; Jas. i. 22); and in the prayer which He dictates to us He bids us ask for the accomplishment of this will as the means of glorifying God, and of sanctifying our souls (Matt. vi. 10).

If thou desirest what is good and art not able to accomplish it, God will reward thee for it as though thou hadst performed it.[57]

He has established as an eternal and unchangeable law that merit should lie in the will, and that upon the will should depend our future of Heaven or hell, reward or punishment.[58]

Charity itself consists in nothing else but a strong will to serve God, a loving desire to please Him, and a fervent longing to enjoy Him.

Finally, He tells us that if we conform ourselves to this sovereign will, we shall be His brethren Matt. xii. 50; Mark iii. 35)

When certain persons, pious or otherwise, confusing sentiment with true love, ask themselves if they love God, or if they will be able to love Him always, we have only to ask them the same question in other words: Are they doing the will of God? can they do it? *i.e.*, can they perform their duty for God's sake? Put thus, the question resolves itself.

The reason for such a doctrine is very simple: to love anyone is to wish him well; that, in the case of God, is to desire His beneficent will towards us. Our Lord and Master recalled this principle when He said to His disciples, "You are My friends, if you do the things that I command you" (John xv. 14).

[57] We must, in virtue of the same principle, keep a firm hold of the truth, as indisputable as it is frequently forgotten, that we have the merit of the good which we will to carry out and are unable to accomplish, as we have also the demerit of the evil we should have done and could not.

[58] "Upon the will depends our future of Heaven or hell," because, given the knowledge of God, the will attaches itself to Him by love, or hates Him with obstinacy.

Forget not, therefore, temptation is not sin, but rather the means of proving virtue. By it man may gain great profit,[59] and this the more inasmuch as "the life of man upon earth is a warfare."[60]

It is by love alone that we turn to God, are transformed into His likeness, and are united to Him, so that we become one spirit with Him, and receive by and from Him all our happiness: here in grace, hereafter in glory. Love can find no rest till she reposes in the full and perfect possession of the Beloved.

It is by the path of love, which is charity, that God draws nigh to man, and man to God, but where charity is not found God cannot dwell. If, then, we possess charity we possess God, for "God is charity."[61]

---

[59] We may notice, in particular, a three-fold benefit: first, temptation calls for conflict, and so strengthens virtue; then it obliges a man to adhere deliberately to that virtue which is assailed by the temptation, and so gain a further perfection; finally, there are necessarily included in both the conflict and the adherence to good numerous virtuous, and therefore meritorious, acts. Thus we may reap advantage from temptation both in our dispositions and our acts.

[60] Job vii. 1.

[61] 1 John iv. 8.

Chapter XII – The Power Of The Love Of God

All that we have hitherto described, all that is necessary for salvation, can find in love alone its highest, completest, most beneficent perfection.

Love supplies all that is wanting for our salvation; it contains abundantly every good thing, and lacks not even the presence of the supreme object of our desires.

There is nothing keener than love, nothing more subtle, nothing more penetrating. Love cannot rest till it has sounded all the depths and learnt the perfections of its Beloved. It desires to be one with Him, and, if it could, would form but one being with the Beloved. It is for this reason that it cannot suffer anything to intervene between it and the object loved, which is God, but springs forward towards Him, and finds no peace till it has overcome every obstacle and reached even unto the Beloved.

Love has the power of uniting and transforming; it transforms the one who loves into him who is loved, and him who is loved into him who loves. Each passes into the other, as far as it is possible.

And first consider the intelligence. How completely love transports the loved one into him who loves! With what sweetness and delight the one lives in the memory of the other, and how earnestly the lover tries to know, not superficially but intimately, all that concerns the object of his love, and strives to enter as far as possible into his inner life!

Think next of the will, by which also the loved one lives in him who loves. Does he not dwell in him by that tender affection, that sweet and deeply-rooted joy which he feels? On the other hand, the lover lives in the beloved by the sympathy of his desires, by sharing his likes and dislikes, his joys and sorrows, until the two seem to form but one. Since "love is strong as death,"[62] it carries the lover out of himself into the heart of the beloved, and holds him prisoner there.

The soul is more truly where it loves than where it gives life, since it exists in the object loved by its own nature, by reason and will; whilst it is in the body it animates only by bestowing on it an existence which it shares with the animal creation.[63]

---

[62] Cant. viii. 6.
[63] The author is speaking here of the soul in so far as it is human, and it is as such that it is more where it loves than where it gives life.

There is, therefore, but one thing which has power to draw us from outward objects into the depths of our own souls, there to form an intimate friendship with Jesus. Nothing but the love of Christ and the desire of His sweetness can lead us thus to feel, to comprehend and experience the presence of His Divinity.

The power of love alone is able to lift up the soul from earth to the heights of Heaven, nor is it possible to ascend to eternal beatitude except on the wings of love and desire.

Love is the life of the soul, its nuptial garment, its perfection.[64]

Upon charity are based the law, the prophets, and the precepts of the Lord.[65] Hence the Apostle wrote to the Romans: "Love is therefore the fulfilling of the law,"[66] and in the first Epistle to Timothy: "The end of the commandment is charity."[67]

---

[64] Without charity there is no perfect virtue, since without it no virtue can lead man to his final end, which is God, although it may lead him to some lower end. It is in this sense that, according to the older theologians, charity is the "form" of the other virtues, since by it the acts of all the other virtues are supernaturalized and directed to their true end--*i.e.*, to God. *Cf.* St. Th. "Sum.," 2, 2{ae}, q. 23, aa. 7, 8.

[65] Matt. xxii. 40.

[66] Rom. xiii. 10.

[67] 1 Tim. i. 5.

Chapter XIII – Of The Nature And Advantages Of Prayer – Of Interior Recollection

Of ourselves we are utterly unable to attain to charity or any other good thing. We have naught to offer to the Lord, the Author of all, which was not His already.

One thing alone remains to us: that in every occurrence we should turn to Him in prayer, as He Himself taught us by word and example. Let us go to Him as guilty, poor, and miserable, as beggars, weak and needy, as subjects and slaves, yet as His children.

Of ourselves we are utterly destitute. What can we do but cast ourselves at His feet in deepest humility, holy fear mingling in our souls with love, peace, and recollection?

And while we are fain to draw nigh with all lowliness and modesty, with minds sincere and simple, let our hearts burn with great desires, with ardour and heartfelt longings. And so let us supplicate our God, and lay before Him with entire confidence the perils which menace us on every side. Let us freely, unhesitatingly, and in all simplicity, confide ourselves to Him, and offer Him our whole being, even to the last fibre, for are we not in truth absolutely His?

Let us keep nothing for ourselves, and then will be fulfilled in us the saying of Saint Isaac, one of the Fathers of the Desert, who, speaking of this kind of prayer, said: "We shall be one being with God, and He will be all in all to us, when that perfect charity by which He loved us first has entered into our inmost hearts."[68]

This will be accomplished when God alone becomes the object of all our love, our desires, our striving, of all our efforts and thoughts, of all that we behold, speak of, hope for; when that union which exists between the Father and the Son, and between the Son and the Father shall be found also in our mind and soul.

Since His love for us is so pure, sincere, and unchanging, ought not we in return to give Him a love constant and uninterrupted?

So, intimate should be our union with Him that our hopes, thoughts, prayers breathe only God.[69] The truly spiritual man should set before him, as the goal of all his efforts and desires, the possession

---

[68] God can only love Himself or creatures for His own sake; if we have this love within our souls we shall be in a certain sense one being with Him.

[69] This teaching is based on the definition that prayer is essentially "an elevation of the soul to God."

even in a mortal body, of an image of the happiness to come, and the enjoyment even here below of some foretaste of the delights, the life, and glory of Heaven.

This, I say, is the end of all perfection--that the soul may become so purified from every earthly longing, and so raised to spiritual things, that at last the whole life and the desires of the heart form one unbroken prayer.

When the soul has thus shaken off the dust of earth and aspires unto her God, to Whom the true religious ever directs his intention, dreading the least separation from Him as a most cruel death; when peace reigns within and she is delivered from the bondage of her passions and cleaves with firmest purpose to the one Sovereign Good, then will be fulfilled in her the words of the Apostle: "Pray without ceasing,"[70] and "in every place, lifting up pure hands, without anger and contention."[71]

When once this purity of soul has gained the victory over man's natural inclination for the things of sense, when all earthly longings are quenched and the soul is, as it were, transformed into the likeness of pure spirits or Angels, then all she

---

[70] 1 Thess. v. 17.
[71] 1 Tim. ii. 8.

receives, all she undertakes, all she does, will be a pure and true prayer.

Only persevere faithfully in thy efforts and, as I have shown from the beginning, it will become as simple and easy for thee to contemplate God and rejoice in Him in thy recollection as to live a purely natural life.

Chapter XIV – That Everything Should Be Judged According To The Testimony Of Our Conscience

There is also another practice which will tend greatly to thy progress in spiritual perfection, and will aid thee to gain purity of soul and tranquil rest in God. Whatever men say or think of thee, bring it before the tribunal of thine own conscience. Enter within thyself, and there, turning a deaf ear to all else, set thyself to learn the truth. Then wilt thou see clearly that the praise and honour of men bring thee no profit, but rather loss, if thou knowest that thou art guilty and worthy of condemnation in the sight of truth. And, just as it is useless to be honoured outwardly by men if thy conscience accuse thee within, so in like manner is it no loss to thee if men despise, blame, or persecute thee without, if within thou art innocent and free from reproach or blame. Nay, rather, thou hast then great reason to rejoice in the Lord in patience, silence, and peace.

Adversity is powerless to harm where sin has no dominion; and just as there is no evil which goes unpunished, so is there no good without recompense.

Seek not with the hypocrites thy reward and crown from men, but rather from the hand of God, not now, but hereafter; not for a passing moment, but for eternity.

Thou canst, therefore, do nothing higher nor better in every tribulation or occurrence than enter into the sanctuary of thy soul, and there call upon the Lord Jesus Christ, thy helper in temptation and affliction. There shouldst thou humble thyself, confessing thy sins, and praising thy God and Father, Who both chastises and consoles.

There dispose thyself to accept with unruffled peace, readiness, and confidence from the hands of God's unfailing Providence and marvellous wisdom all that is sent thee of prosperity or adversity, whether touching thyself or others. Then wilt thou obtain remission of thy sins;[72] bitterness will be driven from thy soul, sweetness and confidence will penetrate it, grace and mercy will descend upon it. Then a sweet familiarity will draw thee on and strengthen thee, abundant consolation will flow to thee from the bosom of God. Then thou wilt adhere to Him and form an indissoluble union with Him.

But beware of imitating hypocrites who, like the Pharisees, try to appear outwardly before men more holy than they know themselves in truth to be. Is it not utter folly to seek or desire human

---

[72] Remission may be obtained in this way of the fault in the case of venial sins, of the punishment due in all sins.

praise and glory for oneself or others, while within we are filled with shameful and grievous sins? Assuredly he who pursues such vanities can hope for no share in the good things of which we spoke just now, but shame will infallibly be his lot.

Keep thy worthlessness and thy sins ever before thine eyes, and learn to know thyself that thou mayest grow in humility.

Shrink not from being regarded by all the world as filthy mud, vile and abject, on account of thy grievous sins and defects. Esteem thyself among others as dross in the midst of gold, as tares in the wheat, straw among the grain, as a wolf among the sheep, as Satan among the children of God.

Neither shouldst thou desire to be respected by others, or preferred to anyone whatsoever. Fly rather with all thy strength of heart and soul from that pestilential poison, the venom of praise, from a reputation founded on boasting and ostentation, lest, as the Prophet says, "The sinner is praised in the desires of his soul."[73]

Again, in Isaias, we read: "They that call thee blessed, the same deceive thee, and destroy the way of thy steps."[74] Also the Lord says: "Woe to you when men shall bless you!"[75]

---

[73] Ps. ix. 24.
[74] Isa. iii. 12.
[75] Luke vi. 26.

Chapter XV – On The Contempt Of Self: How It Is Acquired: Its Profit To The Soul

The more truly a man knows his own misery, the more fully and clearly does he behold the majesty of God. The more vile he is in his own eyes for the sake of God, of truth, and of justice, the more worthy of esteem is he in the eyes of God.

Strive earnestly, therefore, to look on thyself as utterly contemptible, to think thyself unworthy of any benefit, to be displeasing in thine own eyes, but pleasing to God. Desire that others should regard thee as vile and mean.

Learn not to be troubled in tribulations, afflictions, injuries; not to be incensed against those that inflict them, nor to entertain thoughts of resentment against them. Try, on the contrary, sincerely to believe thyself worthy of all injuries, contempt, ill-treatment and scorn.

In truth, he who for God's sake is filled with sorrow and compunction dreads to be honoured and loved by another. He does not refuse to be an object of hatred, or shrink from being trodden under foot and despised as long as he lives, in order that he may practise real humility and cleave in purity of heart to God alone.

It does not require exterior labour or bodily health to love God only, to hate oneself more than all, to desire to seem little in the eyes of others: what is needed is rather repose of the senses, the effort of the heart, silence of the mind.

It is by labouring with the heart, by the inward aspiration of the soul, that thou wilt learn to forsake the base things of earth and to rise to what is heavenly and Divine.

Thus wilt thou become transformed in God, and this the more speedily if, in all sincerity, without condemning or despising thy neighbour, thou desirest to be regarded by all as a reproach and scandal--nay, even to be abhorred as filthy mire, rather than possess the delights of earth, or be honoured and exalted by men, or enjoy any advantage or happiness in this fleeting world.

Have no other desire in this perishable life of the body, no other consolation than unceasingly to weep over, regret and detest thy offences and faults.

Learn utterly to despise thyself, to annihilate thyself and to appear daily more contemptible in the eyes of others.

Strive to become even more unworthy in thine own eyes, in order to please God alone, to love Him only and cling to Him.

Concern not thyself with anything except thy Lord Jesus Christ, Who ought to reign alone in thy affections. Have no solicitude or care save for Him Whose power and Providence give movement and being to all things.[76]

It is not now the time to rejoice but rather to lament with all the sincerity of thy heart.

If thou canst not weep, sorrow at least that thou hast no tears to shed; if thou canst, grieve the more because by the gravity of thy offences and number of thy sins thou art thyself the cause of thy grief. A man under sentence of death does not trouble himself as to the dispositions of his executioners; so he who truly mourns and sheds the tears of repentance, refrains from delight, anger, vainglory, indignation, and every like passion.

---

[76] St. Thomas explains as follows both the possibility and the correctness of this opinion of ourselves: "A man can, without falsehood, believe and declare himself viler than all others, both on account of the secret faults which he knows to exist within him, and on account of the gifts of God hidden in the souls of others." St. Augustine, in his work "De Virginit.," ch. lii., says: "Believe that others are better than you in the depths of their souls, although outwardly you may appear better than they."
In the same way one may truthfully both say and believe that one is altogether useless and unworthy in his own strength. The Apostle says (2 Cor. iii. 5): "Not that we are sufficient to think anything of ourselves, as of ourselves, but our sufficiency is from God" ("Sum.," 2, 2{ae}, q. 161, a. 6, 1{m}).

Citizens and criminals are not lodged in like abodes; so also the life and conduct of those whose faults call for sighs and tears should not resemble those of men who have remained innocent and have nothing to expiate.

Were it otherwise, how would the guilty, great though their crimes may have been, differ in their punishment and expiation from the innocent? Iniquity would then be more free than innocence. Renounce all, therefore, contemn all, separate thyself from all, that thou mayest lay deep the foundations of sincere penance.

He who truly loves Jesus Christ, and sorrows for Him, who bears Him in his heart and in his body, will have no thought, or care, or solicitude for aught else. Such a one will sincerely mourn over his sins and offences, will long after eternal happiness, will remember the Judgment and will think diligently on his last end in lowly fear. He, then, who wishes to arrive speedily at a blessed impassibility and to reach God, counts that day lost on which he has not been ill-spoken of and despised.

What is this impassibility but freedom from the vices and passions, purity of heart, the adornment of virtue?

Count thyself as already dead, since thou must needs die some day.

And now, but one word more. Let this be the test of thy thoughts, words, and deeds. If they render thee more humble, more recollected in God, more strong, then they are according to God. But if thou findest it otherwise, then fear lest all is not according to God, acceptable to Him, or profitable to thyself.

Chapter XVI – Of The Providence Of God, Which Watches Over All Things

Wouldst thou draw nigh unto God without let or hindrance, freely and in peace, as we have described? Desirest thou to be united and drawn to Him in a union so close that it will endure in prosperity and adversity, in life and in death? Delay not to commit all things with trustful confidence into the hands of His sure and infallible Providence.

Is it not most fitting that thou shouldst trust Him Who gives to all creatures, in the first place, their existence, power, and movement, and, secondly, their species and nature, ordering in all their number, weight, and measure?

Just as Art presupposes the operations of Nature, so Nature presupposes the work of God, the Creator, Preserver, Organizer, and Administrator.

To Him alone belong infinite power, wisdom, and goodness, essential mercy, justice, truth, and charity, immutable eternity, and immensity. Nothing can exist and act of its own power, but every creature acts of necessity by the power of

God, the first moving cause, the first principle and origin of every action, Who acts in every active being.

If we consider the ordered harmony of the universe, it is the Providence of God which must arrange all things, even to the smallest details.

From the infinitely great to the infinitely small nothing can escape His eternal Providence; nothing has been drawn from His control, either in the acts of free-will, in events we ascribe to chance or fate, or in what has been designed by Him. We may go further: it is as impossible for God to make anything which does not fall within the dominion of His Providence as it is for Him to create anything which is not subject to His action. Divine Providence, therefore, extends over all things, even the thoughts of man.

This is the teaching of Holy Scripture, for in the Epistle of St. Peter it is written: "Casting all your care upon Him, for He hath care of you."[77]

And, again, the Prophet says: "Cast thy care upon the Lord and He shall sustain thee."[78] Also in Ecclesiasticus we read: "My children, behold the generations of men; and know ye that no one hath hoped in the Lord, and hath been confounded. For

---

[77] 1 Pet. v. 7.
[78] Ps. liv. 23.

who hath continued in His commandment, and hath been forsaken?"[79] And the Lord says: "Be not solicitous, therefore, saying, What shall we eat?"[80] All that thou canst hope for from God, however great it may be, thou shalt without doubt receive, according to the promise in Deuteronomy: "Every place that your foot shall tread upon shall be yours."[81] As much as thou canst desire thou shalt receive, and as far as the foot of thy confidence reaches, so far thou shalt possess.

Hence St. Bernard says: "God, the Creator of all things, is so full of mercy and compassion that whatever may be the grace for which we stretch out our hands, we shall not fail to receive it."[82]

It is written in St. Mark: "Whatsoever ye shall ask when ye pray, believe that you shall receive, and they shall come unto you."[83]

The greater and more persistent thy confidence in God, and the more earnestly thou turnest to Him in lowly reverence, the more abundantly and certainly shalt thou receive all thou dost hope and ask.

---

[79] Ecclus. ii. 11, 12.
[80] Matt. vi. 31.
[81] Deut. xi. 24.
[82] *Cf.* Serm. I. in Pent.
[83] Mark xi. 24.

But if, on account of the number and magnitude of his sins, the confidence of any should languish, let him who feels this torpor remember that all is possible to God, that what He wills must infallibly happen, and what He wills not cannot come to pass, and, finally, that it is as easy for Him to forgive and blot out innumerable and heinous sins as to forgive one.

On the other hand, it is just as impossible for a sinner to deliver himself from a single sin as it would be for him to raise and cleanse himself from many sins; for, not only are we unable to accomplish this, but of ourselves we cannot even think what is right.[84] All comes to us from God. It is, however, far more dangerous, other things being equal, to be entangled in many sins than to be held only by one.

In truth, no evil remains unpunished, and for every mortal sin is due, in strict justice, an infinite punishment, because a mortal sin is committed against God, to Whom belong infinite greatness, dignity, and glory.

Moreover, according to the Apostle, "the Lord knoweth who are His,"[85] and it is impossible that one of them should perish, no matter how violently the tempests and waves of error rage, how great the

---

[84] 2 Cor. iii. 5.
[85] 2 Tim. ii. 19.

scandal, schisms and persecutions, how grievous the adversities, discords, heresies, tribulations, or temptations of every kind.

The number of the elect and the measure of their merit is eternally and unalterably predestined. So true is this that all the good and evil which can happen to them or to others, all prosperity and adversity, serve only to their advantage.

Nay more, adversity does but render them more glorious, and proves their fidelity more surely.

Delay not, therefore, to commit all things without fear to the Providence of God, by Whose permission all evil of whatever kind happens, and ever for some good end. It could not be except He permitted it; its form and measure are allowed by Him Who can and will by His wisdom turn all to good.

Just as it is by His action that all good is wrought, so is it by His permission that all evil happens.[86]

---

[86] The teaching of Albert the Great on Divine Providence is truly admirable. It is based upon the axiom that the actions of the creature do not depend partly upon itself and partly upon God, but wholly upon itself and wholly upon God (*cf.* St. Thomas "Cont. Gent.," iii. 70).

Human causality is not parallel with the Divine, but subordinate to it, as the scholastics teach. This doctrine alone safeguards the action of God and of that of the creature. The doctrine of parallelism derogates from both, and leads to fatalism by attributing to God things which He has not done, and suppressing

But from the evil He draws good, and thus marvellously shows forth His power, wisdom, and clemency by our Lord Jesus Christ. So also He manifests His mercy and His justice, the power of grace, the weakness of nature, and the beauty of the universe. So He shows by the force of contrast the glory of the good, and the malice and punishment of the wicked.

In like manner, in the conversion of a sinner we behold contrition, confession, and penance; and, on the other hand, the tenderness of God, His mercy and charity, His glory and His goodness.

Yet sin does not always turn to the good of those who commit it; but it is usually the greatest of perils and worst of ills, for it causes the loss of grace and glory. It stains the soul and provokes chastisement and even eternal punishment. From so great an evil may our Lord Jesus vouchsafe to preserve us! Amen.

---

for man the necessary principle of all good, especially that of liberty.

It is the doctrine of subordinated causes also which explains how things decreed by God are determined by the supreme authority, and infallibly come to pass, without prejudice to the freedom of action of secondary causes. All this belongs to the highest theology. Unhappily, certain modern authors have forgotten it.

AN EASY METHOD
OF
MENTAL PRAYER

by

Father Bertrand Wilberforce, O.P.

I. What Mental Prayer is

Prayer is, says St. Gregory Nazianzen, a conference or conversation with God, St. John Chrysostom calls it a discoursing with the Divine Majesty; according to St. Augustine it is the raising up of the soul to God. St. Francis of Sales describes it as a conversation of the soul with God, by which we speak to God and He to us, by which we aspire to Him, and breathe in Him, and He in return inspires us and breathes on us.

All prayer then is the speaking of the soul to God. This may be done in three ways; for the prayer may be either in thought only, unexpressed in any external way, or on the other hand the secret thoughts and feelings of the soul may be clothed in words; and these words again may either be confined to a set form, or they may be words of our own, unfettered by any form and expressing the emotions of our soul at the moment. In the first case our prayer will be purely mental; in the second, in which we employ a set form of words, it will be vocal prayer; in the third case, where the prayer is chiefly in thought, but these thoughts are allowed to break forth into words in any way that at the moment seem best to express the feelings of the soul, it is a mixture of mental and vocal prayer;

but as the words are spontaneous and not in any prescribed form, it may justly be considered as mental prayer.

In an audience with the Pope, we might read a written address to His Holiness, or we might trust to the words that might occur at the moment to express what we desired to convey to his mind. But if God were to enable the Pope to read the thoughts of our mind, we might then simply stand silent in his presence, and he would see all that we wanted to express. The formal address would be vocal prayer, the silent standing before his throne would be purely mental prayer, the conversation with unprepared words would be a mixture of the two and might be called mental prayer in a more general and extended sense. God knows our secret thoughts more clearly than we can express them, more certainly than we ourselves can know them; and words therefore are not necessary in our intercourse with Him, though often a considerable help to us.

A set form of words spoken or read cannot be called prayer at all unless the mind intends it as prayer and gives some kind spiritual attention, either to the actual sense of the words themselves or to God Himself while they are uttered. Shakespeare spoke as a theologian when, in Hamlet, he put into the mouth of the King, who asked for pardon without repentance:

My words go up, my thoughts remain below; Words without thoughts never to heaven go.

God condemned the merely material homage of the Jews by declaring, "This people honoureth Me with their lips, but their heart is far from Me." All prayer, therefore, of whatever kind, must be "in spirit and in truth" [St. John iv, 23]; but vocal prayer is confined to a prescribed form of words, whereas mental prayer is the spontaneous utterance of the soul either with or without words. When St. Francis of Assisi said an Our Father, or recited his office, he used vocal prayer; when he knelt before God without a word, his prayer was purely mental; when he spent the whole night in saying "My God and my all", his mental prayer was mingled with words which expressed the burning love of his seraphic soul.

II. The Importance and Necessity of Mental Prayer

Prayer of one kind or another is absolutely and indispensably necessary for salvation – in other words, no one who has come to the use of reason, so as to be capable of prayer, can, according to God's ordinary providence, be saved without it. This necessity is proved in the first place from the distinct, emphatic and constantly repeated command to pray, and to pray continually. For instance. "He spoke a parable to them (to show) that we ought always to pray, and not to faint"[87]; "Watch and pray, that ye enter not into temptation"[88]: "Ask, and it shall be given you"[89] : "Be instant (that is earnest) in prayer"[90], and "Pray without ceasing"[91].

Besides these positive commands it is evidently necessary; because though God really wills the salvation of all,[92] , He will not save us without our own co-operation. He will save no one by force: for heaven is not the land of slaves. into which men are

---

[87] St Luke xviii, 1
[88] St Matt. xxvi, 41
[89] St. Matt. vii, 7
[90] Coloss. iv, 2
[91] I Thess. v, 17
[92] 1 Tim. li. 4

driven by compulsion; it is the home of the free children of God, of those who love God, of those who are free with the freedom with which Christ hath made us free. Therefore, God gives to all the grace to pray; and if they use this grace and continue to pray aright, He will continue to bestow on them a chain of graces that will end in salvation. But to those who will not pray, He has promised nothing: "The Lord is nigh unto all that call upon Him; to all that call upon Him in truth"[93]. "Draw nigh to God, and He will draw nigh to you".[94]

From this absolute and indispensable necessity of prayer in general, we can easily infer the importance and the moral necessity of the best and highest kind of prayer – namely mental prayer. If not absolutely, it is certainly morally necessary in some form or another even for salvation; and there can be no manner of doubt that it is strictly necessary for any real advance of the soul in virtue and divine love. St. Alphonsus says : "He who neglects meditation (a part of mental prayer), and is distracted by the affairs of the world, will not know his spiritual wants, the dangers to which his salvation is exposed, the means he ought to take to conquer temptations; and will forget the necessity of the prayer of petition for all men: thus he will not

[93] Ps. cxliv, 18
[94] St. James iv, 8

ask for what is necessary, and by not asking God's grace, he will certainly lose his soul."

In the same way St. Teresa asks: "How can charity last, unless God gives perseverance? How will the Lord give us perseverance if we neglect to ask Him for it? And how shall we ask it without mental prayer? Without mental prayer there is not the communication with God which is necessary for the preservation of virtue." The holy Doctors agree that those who persevere in mental prayer will live in God's grace. The following words are the deliberate sentence of the holy Doctor St. Alphonsus, the conclusion gathered from his vast learning and experience: "Many say the Rosary, the Office of Our Lady, and other acts of devotion, but they still continue in sin. But it is impossible for him who perseveres in mental prayer to continue in sin: he will either give up mental prayer or renounce sin. Mental prayer and sin cannot exist together. And this we see by experience; they who make mental prayer rarely fall into mortal sin; and should they have the misery of falling into sin, by persevering in mental prayer they see their misery and return to God. Let a soul, says St. Teresa, be ever so negligent; if she perseveres in mental prayer the Lord will bring her back to the haven of salvation."

If this were merely the opinion of St. Alphonsus himself, it would be of immense weight, considering his resplendent sanctity, his vast spiritual learning, and the varied experience of his long and active life; but besides this the holy Doctor is here only summing up in one sentence the teaching and experience of all the doctors, saints, writers, preachers, and confessors of the whole Church since the beginning. What stronger argument could be used to prove the importance and necessity of mental prayer?

III. Is Mental Prayer Easy?

Anyone who has a real desire to be saved, and who believes that the opinion of St. Alphonsus and all other spiritual teachers – that mortal sin and mental prayer cannot live together, but are mutually destructive – is really true, but must feel a desire to adopt so certain a means of salvation. But many are fainthearted and dread the little difficulty they feel in beginning a new exercise; and many more lack the courage and self-denial necessary to continue in it after the novelty has worn away, and the yoke of perseverance begins to gall. Blessed are they who courageously persevere, for their salvation is secure!

Those who find it difficult to begin or are tempted to abandon this powerful means of salvation, must pluck up heart, and encourage themselves by remembering that mental prayer requires no learning, no special power of mind, no extraordinary grace, but only a resolute will and a desire to please God. In fact, the hard matter is to convince people how easy and simple a matter mental prayer really is, and that the difficulty is far more imaginary than real. This difficulty often rises from not having grasped the true idea of what is meant by mental prayer; and the false idea of the exercise, once formed, is often never corrected, the consequence being that the practice is either abandoned in disgust or persevered in with extreme repugnance and little fruit.

One common cause of misunderstanding, perhaps the most common of all, is the custom of calling the whole exercise by the name of one subordinate and not the most important part - that is meditation. From this the idea arises that it is a prolonged spiritual study, drawn out at length with many divisions and much complicated process; and this notion frightens many good souls, and makes them fall back on vocal prayer alone. They imagine that the soul must preach a discourse to itself. and they feel no talent for preaching. Many, if they spoke their minds clearly, would say: "I cannot meditate, but if I might be allowed to pray during that time instead, I could do very well." This is no imaginary case. as anyone who has had any experience will testify, and this miserable misunderstanding, that so often holds souls back for years, is partly brought about by defective teaching, but partly also by the name *meditation* being used instead of the more comprehensive one of *mental prayer*.

Mental prayer, properly understood, will be found to be easy and within the power of all who desire salvation. Of course, there are many degrees of prayer, and to pray perfectly is no doubt a matter of great difficulty; but to pray well, and in a way very pleasing to God and very profitable to the soul, is an easy and simple manner. If we remember how many thousands have excelled in mental prayer, though not even able to read, we shall see that this holy exercise cannot require any special power of mind or any degree of culture. St. Isidore, a farm laborer, is an example of a man utterly devoid of human learning, but rising, by God's grace, to the sublimest prayer.

The following method of making mental prayer is drawn from the works of St. Alphonsus who may justly be called the Doctor of Prayer; and it is so simple that no one who studies it with any attention can fail to understand it, and all who reduce it to practice will find that in great measure it takes away the difficulty they may feel in the exercise. Many who have found "making a meditation" to be a wearisome penance, have experienced that with this method the time is all too short: and that conversation with God is indeed the greatest joy of life; "Taste and see how sweet the Lord is."

IV. Method of Mental Prayer

All methods of mental prayer are essentially the same. They are different ways of reaching the same end, the object of all being to teach the soul how she can converse lovingly with God. In the method recommended by St. Alphonsus, the whole exercise is divided into three parts – the Preparation, the Body of the Prayer, and the Conclusion.

i. Preparation

The real preparation for prayer is a good life, a spirit of recollection enabling a man to live in God's presence, and the invaluable habit of regular spiritual reading. But this is not the place to enter into these matters, and so we must proceed to the immediate preparation, when the time of prayer has come. "Before prayer prepare thy soul and be not as a man that tempteth God"[95]. From this admonition of the Holy Ghost, it is evident that we must not presume to throw ourselves down before God unprepared, our minds full of idle, distracting thoughts, and imagine that we can thus pray in a way pleasing to Him. How careful should we be to prepare both body and mind if admitted to a papal or a royal audience! At least then make in preparation for your conference with God, three short though fervent acts:

1. An act of faith in God's presence, and of adoration, profound and humble, of His majesty.

2. An act of contrition for sin, sin forming the cloud thick and dark over our heads that hides the brightness of God's face. "Your sins have hid his face from you"[96].

---

[95] Eccles. xviii, 23
[96] Isaiah lix, 2

3. A fervent petition for light to see God's holy will, especially in some one matter either pressing upon us then or suggested by the subject we are going to consider, and for grace to do God's will when we do see it.

Examples of these acts may help beginners, but it must be clearly understood that they are only examples and that they may be made in any form.

1. Adoration of God present in your soul:

My God, I believe that Thou art present with me and within me, and I adore Thee with all the affection of any soul, "Be watchful," says St. Alphonsus, "to make this act with a lively faith, for the remembrance of the presence of God is a great help to keep away distractions." Cardinal Carracciolo, Bishop of Aversa, used to say that distractions are a sign that the soul has not made a lively act of faith.

2. Sorrow for sin, our sins preventing union with God in prayer:

O Lord by my sins I deserve now to be in hell; I repent, O infinite Goodness, with my whole heart of having offended Thee. I am sorry for sin from the bottom of my heart; have mercy on me.

3. Ask for light:

O Eternal Father, for the love of Jesus and Mary, give me light in this prayer, that I may profit by it.

Then add a Hail Mary, an ejaculation to St. Joseph, your Guardian Angel, and your holy patrons.

These acts should be short. In a mental prayer of half-an-hour, not more than three minutes should be devoted to them. But at the same time, they should be fervent and earnest, the whole attention being given to them; for upon the manner in which they are made will, in great measure, depend the fervor of the whole prayer.

ii. Body of the Prayer

In order to pray with fruit and without distraction, it is very useful, and in most cases necessary, to spend some time in meditation or pious thought, on some definite subject; and from this fact, as before stated, the whole exercise is often called meditation. Instead of mental prayer. This often misleads people into imagining that meditation, that is, the use of the intellect in thinking on a holy subject, the main end to be aimed at, whereas in fact it is prayer, or conversation with God. Meditation furnishes us with the matter for conversation, but it is not itself prayer at all. When thinking and reflecting, the soul speaks to itself, reasons with itself; in prayer it speaks to God.

Meditation, in its wide sense, is any kind of attentive and repeated thought upon any subject and with any intention; but in the more restricted sense in which it is understood as a part of mental prayer, it is, as St. Francis of Sales puts it, "an attentive thought, voluntarily repeated or entertained in the mind, to excite the will to holy and salutary reflections and resolutions". It differs in its object from mere study: we study to improve our minds and to store up information; we meditate to move the will to pray and to embrace good. We study that we may know, we meditate that we may pray.

We must then use the mind in thus thinking of or pondering on a sacred subject for a few minutes; and in order to help the mind in this exercise, we must have some definite subject of thought, upon which it is well to read either a text of Holy Scripture, or a few lines out of some other holy book. St. Teresa tells us that she thus helped herself with a book for seventeen years. By this short reading, the mind is rendered attentive and is set on a train of thought. Further to help the mind, you can ask yourself some such questions as the following: What does this mean? What lesson does it teach me? What have I done about this in the past? What shall I now do, and how?

Two remarks are here most important.

The first is, that care must be taken not to read too much but to stop when any thought strikes the mind. If the reading is prolonged, if for example, in a short prayer of half-an-hour you were to read for ten minutes, the exercise would be changed into spiritual reading.

The second remark is, that you must not be distressed if you find the mind torpid, and if only one or two very simple thoughts present themselves. It is by no means necessary to have many thoughts, nor to indulge in deep and well-arranged reflections. The object of mental prayer is not to preach a well-prepared and eloquent sermon to yourself, the object is to pray. If one simple thought makes you pray, why distress yourself because you have not other and more elaborate thoughts? If you wanted to reach the top of a roof, you would not trouble yourself because your ladder was a short one, provided it was long enough to land you safely on the roof. The end is gained. If one simple reflection enables you to pray, you would, in reality, be merely distracting yourself from prayer, in order to occupy yourself with your own thoughts, if you were to go on developing a lengthy train of thought. This would be to mistake the means for the end, and it is a very common mistake, and the cause of great discouragement. This mistake will be evident if you remember that while you are following out a line of thought, for instance, when you are answering the questions suggested above you are conversing with yourself.

It is plain therefore that as your object is to converse with God, you should not remain too long in talking to yourself, and that therefore, if you feel a difficulty in doing this, you need not be distressed. "The progress of a soul," says the enlightened St. Teresa, "does not consist in thinking much of God, but in loving Him ardently; and this love is gained by resolving to do a great deal for Him."

I have said that misunderstanding this point is the most fruitful source of discouragement and one of the commonest reasons for abandoning mental prayer in disgust; and the reason is, because very few people are accustomed to prolonged or deep thought on any - subject few indeed are capable of it. If therefore they imagine that prolonged if not deep thought, is necessary for mental prayer, they are in constant trouble and discouragement, which ends in their abandoning the whole exercise in despair. "If I might only be allowed to pray," they will sigh to themselves," how much easier it would be!"

Let such persons then clearly understand that many thoughts are not necessary, that their reflections need not be deep and ought not, especially in a prayer of half-an-hour, to be long, lest prayer should be neglected, and the exercise be changed into a study. "Meditation," says St. Alphonsus, "is the needle which only passes through so that it may draw after it the golden thread, which is composed of affections, petitions and resolutions." The needle is only used in order to draw the thread after it. If then you were to meditate for an hour and think out a subject in all its details, but without constant acts and petitions, you would be working hard with an unthreaded needle.

Men's minds differ as much as their features, and some men, especially those employed in very distracting duties, need more thought than others before they can pray; but many, especially women, will find that the effort, after prolonged reflections, will generally defeat itself, and end in distraction.

As soon, therefore, as you feel an impulse to pray, give way to it at once in the best way you can by acts and petitions, in other words. begin your conversation with God on the subject about which you have been thinking. Do not imagine, moreover, that it is necessary to wait for a great fire to burn up in your soul but cherish the little spark that you have got. Above all, never give way to the mistaken notion that you must restrain yourself from prayer in order to go through all the thoughts suggested by your book, or because your prayer does not appear to have a close connection with the subject of your meditation. This would simply be to run from God to your own thoughts, or to those of some other man.

One useful suggestion may here be introduced. Those who are accustomed to make regular spiritual reading will often meet some idea, or passage of their author, which strikes their mind forcibly, or seems especially suited for their own practice. When this is the case, they could not do better than to take that idea, or that passage, as the subject of their next mental prayer. As they have read about it and thought about it in the time of spiritual reading, a very slight reflection will be enough to enable them to pray upon that subject with solid fruit, and to make practical resolutions concerning it.

We have spoken thus far of the needle: now we must proceed to consider the golden thread, which is the matter of principal importance, and should occupy the chief part of the time devoted to prayer. The golden thread is composed of a) acts or affections of the will, b) petitions and c) resolutions: a triple cord of beauty and strength, which, when the soul uses earnestly, she can be said to have "girded her loins with strength and strengthened her arm."[97].

a) Acts or Affections Of The Will

Acts, or affections of the will, are the movements of the soul towards God. The affections are called the feet of the soul, because by them she approaches to or recedes from God. To "draw nigh to God" does not mean any bodily motion, but the spiritual progression of love. When therefore in meditating on a subject you feel some holy sentiment arising in your heart, begin to make simple acts, with or without words, to God. Acts of this nature are very various, such as faith, hope, confidence, humility, thanksgiving, contrition, love. They should be simple, short, and often repeated. Think of our Lord's prayer in the Garden, which is intended as a model to us. He prayed for three hours, and His whole prayer consisted in the constant repetition of one single act of resignation and petition. The word "ACTS" will suggest the chief aspirations, that it is well constantly to repeat A stands for

---

[97] Prov. xxxi, 17

Adoration; C for Contrition; T for Thanksgiving, to which is joined love; and S for Supplication, the prayer of petition.

These acts should be spontaneous, springing up from your own soul, but some examples may help beginners. If then you were to take as the subject of your prayer the death of our Lord Jesus Christ on the Cross, you would, after the preparatory acts, begin to think of the mystery. "Who is that hanging on the Cross?"- you would say to yourself – "What is He suffering – in body, in soul? Why does He suffer?"

Not many minutes thought would be necessary before you would feel moved to acts of Faith: "O my Lord, hanging on the Cross, I believe in Thee. Thou art the Eternal God, made man for me. Thou art my Redeemer; for my sins Thou art thus bleeding and dying on the Cross," etc.

Humility: "O my Jesus, I am not worthy to live. I have slain Thee, the Son of God. Who am I, dear Lord, that Thou, the everlasting God, hast thus suffered and died for me! I am Thy creature, made by Thy Hands. I am Thy rebellious child. I deserve hell for my sins, I deserve to have been abandoned by Thee, and yet Thou hast thought of me and hast offered Thyself as a victim for me. How good Thou art, dear Lord, to be nailed to the Cross for so miserable and ungrateful a sinner! I will not sin again," etc.

Confidence: "If I look at myself, dear Lord, l am filled with fear. I have sinned, O Lord, against Thee, my sins are more in number than the hairs of my head. How shall I dare ever to hope for pardon, after having so often and so basely offended Thee! But Thy death is my hope. Thou hast made me, I am Thine, and Thou hast suffered for me, and died for me. I hope in Thee, in Thee do I put my trust, and I shall not be confounded forever. Thou canst not reject me now that I repent, when Thou hast shed Thy Blood for me," etc.

Thanksgiving: "l thanks Thee. O Lord, with all my heart for Thy great goodness in dying for me and shedding all Thy Blood for me. Blessed be Thy holy Name! I thank Thee for not abandoning me when I committed that sin, for loving me in spite of all my many sins against Thee. Blessed be Jesus, who shed His precious Blood for me! Most holy Mary, help me to thank thy Son for all He has done for me," etc.

Contrition: "I am heartily sorry for all my sins. I detest them all, and especially because they have displeased Thee, because they have nailed Thee to the Cross. Lord, be merciful to me, a sinner! Father, forgive me, for I knew not what I did," etc.

Love: "I love Thee. my Jesus. I love Thee. but I do not love Thee as I ought; make me love Thee more and more. I love Thee with my whole heart. I desire to see Thee loved by all. I will only what Thou willest. Thou hast died for love of me. I desire to die for love of Thee: I rejoice that Thou art eternally happy. Do with me and all that is mine according to Thy will". "This last act of love and oblation of self," says St. Alphonsus, "is especially pleasing to God, and St. Teresa used thus to offer herself to God at least fifty times in the day."

Acts of love should be frequent whatever the subject of meditation may have been.

"The act of love", continues the same Saint, "as also the act of contrition (which is sorrow founded on love) is the golden chain which binds the soul to God." An act of perfect charity is sufficient for the remission of all our sins: "Charity covereth a multitude of sins"[98].

The Ven. Sister Mary of the Crucified once saw, in a vision, a globe of fire, in the flames of which straws were instantly burnt up. She was thus made to understand that when the soul makes acts of love to God, all her sins are consumed in the flames of charity and are forgiven. Besides, the Angelic Doctor, St. Thomas, teaches that by every act of

---

[98] I Pet. iv, 8

love, we gain a fresh degree of glory. "Every act of charity merits eternal life." How many we can make in the course of the day, if we have some little fervor, especially during the time of mental prayer!

St. Francis of Sales has the following consoling and most instructive words concerning acts of sorrow founded on love, or, as he styles them, acts of loving repentance. "Because this loving repentance is ordinarily practiced by elevations and raisings of the heart to God, like to those of the ancient penitents: I am Thine, save me! Have mercy on me, O God, have mercy on me, for my soul trusteth in Thee. Save me, O God; for the waters are come in even unto my soul. Make me as one of Thy hired servants. O God be merciful to me a sinner."

It is not without reason that some have said that prayer justifies; for the repentant prayer or the suppliant repentance raising up the soul to God and reuniting it to His goodness, without doubt obtains pardon, in virtue of the holy love which gives it the sacred movement. And therefore, we ought all to have very many such ejaculatory prayers, made in the sense of a loving repentance and of sighs which seek our reconciliation with God; so that by these laying our tribulation before our Savior, we may pour out our souls before and within His pitiful heart, which will receive them to mercy"[99].

As already stated, these acts or affections should spring from the heart; we must not look for fine words nor make up grand sentences; the mere movement of the will towards God, with love, gratitude, hope, sorrow for sin, etc, is sufficient even without words. Therefore, does our Lord say: "Do not speak much when you pray"- a simple movement of the heart is better than many words proceeding merely from the lips. Nor should we hurry from one affection to another. If you feel yourself moved to make acts of love, keep on making acts of love; if you are excited to sorrow, repeat acts of sorrow for a while, till the affections grow cold; then pass on to another. Moreover, these affections should be made slowly, allowing the soul to dwell upon each act. It is well to make slight pauses between. God often speaks to us during these pauses, and when He does, when we perceive some good thought in our mind giving us some new light, a clearer insight into ourselves or a better knowledge of God or showing us our duty or God's will for us, then we should listen humbly while God speaks, prepared to obey His commands.

---

[99] Treatise on the Love of God Book ii, chap. XX

b) Petitions

Besides the acts and affections of the soul, all of which are truly prayer, since the soul, in making them, converses with God, it is extremely useful to occupy ourselves during mental prayers in making many fervent petitions to God for His spiritual graces and favor.

This prayer of petition is a matter that St. Alphonsus, in all his ascetical works, is continually urging upon every soul in language the most emphatic. Indeed, our Lord Himself has given us the first lesson as to the necessity of constant petition, not only by His command, "Ask and it shall be given unto you," but by the fact that the Our Father, the model of all prayers, consists half of affections and half of petitions for what we need. In English, we have not any one word that expresses this kind of prayer, and we are obliged to call it prayer of petition. The French word *la prière* expresses it, while *l'oraison* means mental prayer with its acts, affections, and resolutions. This distinction explains many passages in the works of St. Alphonsus – for instance, where he says, "Without prayer (that is, petitions for graces) all the meditations we make, all our resolutions, all our promises will be useless. If we do not pray (that is, if we do not make petitions for graces) we shall always be unfaithful to the inspirations of God, and to the promises we make Him. Because in order actually to do good, to conquer temptations, to practice virtues, and to observe God's law, it is not enough to receive light from God, and to meditate and to make resolutions, but we require moreover the actual assistance of God, and He does not give this assistance except to those who pray and pray with perseverance" (Treatise on Prayer Part I).

Here is the distinction between meditation with resolutions, or mental prayer in general, and prayer of petition, or between *l'oraison* and *la prière*.

Without this distinction. which is not at first apparent in English translations, much that is said of prayer is confusing and unintelligible. For instance. in the above extract the Saint appears to say that mental prayer without prayer is of no avail. Again in his "Rule of Life for a Christian" in that most valuable volume called "The Christian Virtues", the second rule is about mental prayer while the sixth is concerning prayer. When we understand that prayer means prayer of petition, the difficulty vanishes. In his constant exhortations to the practice of prayer of petition, the holy Doctor is fond of quoting the experience of that learned and enlightened writer Fr. Paul Segneri. S.J., who thus speaks of himself: "When I began and before I had studied theology, I used to employ my time of mental prayer in reflections and affections; but God opened my eyes afterwards. and from that time, I endeavored to occupy myself in petitions, and if there is any good in me I consider it to be due to this habit of recommending myself to God."

Petitions, therefore, for all you need, are a very important part of mental prayer, and are most useful to the soul. But a caution is necessary here to prevent misunderstanding. The petitions in the time of mental prayer should be spiritual petitions – that is, for spiritual objects, such as forgiveness of sin, love of God, light to see, and grace to do God's will.

For if the petitions were for temporal favors, such as health of body for yourself or others, success in business, rain or fine weather and the like, two inconveniences would follow:

— In the first place it is always doubtful whether such things are according to the will of God or not, and they must be asked for only if they should be the Divine Will, and the whole spiritual value of the petition will then be in that act of resignation.

— Secondly, the mind be much distracted from God in order to think of the matters upon which to form petitions, and especially if the subject of the petition should be some person in whose temporal welfare you are much interested, or some worldly business that gives you anxiety, to pray for these things would probably result in distraction. The mind would begin to reflect upon the things themselves and forget God.

By this, it is not meant that these temporal matters must never be made the subject of prayer, but only that it is not generally advisable to occupy the mind with them during mental prayer, for the reasons given. The truth is that all these things are suggestions from experience; for in the matter of mental prayer, in which "the Spirit bloweth where He listeth," there are very few "musts," few things of which you can say this must be done.

With this understanding as to the subject matter of petitions, the soul cannot be better occupied during mental prayer than in making frequent and earnest petitions, in the name of our Lord Jesus Christ, for all the graces she feels to need. Ask, then, for help in the time of temptation, beg grace always to persevere in prayer when tempted, but particularly remember always to pray for the three following graces, which, if you obtain, will render your salvation secure. These three all-important graces are:

* (a) The perfect forgiveness of past sin.

* (b) The perfect love of God.

* (c) The grace of a holy death.

Christ our Lord, Truth itself, has promised distinctly and emphatically, "Ask, and it shall be given you; seek, and you shall find; knock, and it shall be opened unto you."[100]. "All things whatsoever you shall ask in prayer, believing, you shall receive."[101]. Ask then for these three graces, which, by their very nature, must be according to God's will that you shall have; ask for them with humility, confidence, and perseverance, and they must be given to you. God's promise cannot fail. Ask for the perfect forgiveness of all your sins, and, however many and grievous they may have been, forgiveness will be yours. Seek for the love of God by many earnest petitions, and you shall find it. Knock at Heaven's gate by constant petition for a holy death, and the golden gate of that city of love and peace will be opened to you, as your eyes close in death, and your soul departs into eternity. "Pray," exclaims St. Alphonsus, "pray, and never give up praying. If you pray, you will certainly be saved; if you do not pray, you will certainly be lost." We have so many spiritual wants, that half-an-hour's prayer will be all too short to make our earnest petitions before the throne of mercy.

---

[100] St. Matt. v ii, 7
[101] St. Matt. xxi, 22

c) Resolutions

In order to make mental prayer truly fruitful, you should be careful to make some definite and precise resolution, either to avoid some fault or to practice some virtue. Mere thought, it is evident, cannot make us holy. Acts and affections by themselves will not make us practice virtue. Even petitions by themselves are not enough. They obtain for us, it is true, the strength to conquer sin. and to do what is good; but the most difficult matter remains – that is, to use this grace, and actually, to do what we recognize to be God's will.

We must, then, make a resolution to carry in practice what we see to be good. How frequently, from want of this steadfast resolution, men pray for a grace, but in their actions deny and contradict their prayers! The resolution should be often repeated, day after day, until we can easily keep faithful to it. Moreover, it should be definite, that is, not too general and vague. A determination for instance, to be better than we have hitherto been, to be humble, to love God, is of no practical advantage whatever. It means nothing, it will begin and end itself, and produce no effect on our daily life; we must therefore resolve to avoid some particular fault into which we are likely to fall that day, or to practice some one act of virtue that very day.

The resolution moreover must be of a practical nature, that is, it must be something that we can do if we please; and above all, it must be sincere, by which is meant that we must truly intend in our hearts to carry it into practice when the opportunity occurs. It may be perfectly sincere at the time, even if we are weak enough afterwards to fail in its practice, but there is no excuse if we are insincere at the time of making it. That would surely be insulting to God, who sees the heart. We must never forget 'he words of St. Teresa, already quoted "The progress of a soul does not consist in thinking much of God, but in loving Him ardently, and this love is gained by resolving to do a great deal for him." Make then one practical definite resolution that you can keep and mean to keep that very day.

iii. Conclusion of the prayer

Before rising from your knees, three short but fervent acts should be made, as the finishing stroke of your mental prayer.

1. An act of thanksgiving for the lights and graces that God has given you during your prayer. For instance: "I thank Thee, O my God, in the name of Jesus Christ, for all the help Thou hast given me. Blessed be Thy holy name. Glory be to the Father," etc.

2. Renew earnestly the good resolution you have already made.

3. Ask for grace to keep it.

You can address this petition either to the Eternal Father, begging Him through the merits of Jesus and the intercession of Mary, to grant you this favor; or you can address our Lord Himself, or you can beg the prayers of our Lady or your patrons.

Lastly, make an ejaculation for the conversion of sinners, and for the souls in purgatory.

V. Concluding Remarks

A few concluding remarks may be useful, in order to remove difficulties that often arise and discourage the souls who feel drawn to give themselves to the holy and delightful exercise of prayer.

1. "Is not mental prayer a very complicated manner? There seems so much to remember, so many things to do!"

When the method of prayer is drawn out step by step on paper this is quite true. It does look a complicated affair, and so would everything else if it were thus minutely described. Try to set down on paper all that we must remember in order to eat and drink in a polite manner and see how formal and complicated it all seems; but do it, and it at once appears easy and natural. It is the same with mental prayer. Practice it for a short time, and all its difficulty will vanish.

2. "Are all these things to be done in the exact order prescribed?"

The preparation will always come first, with the three short fervent acts, and the conclusion will always naturally be at the end; but in the body of the prayer no formal order is to be observed. That part should indeed always begin by a short meditation, some simple earnest thoughts, but the acts and petitions should come forth from the heart in any way that they arise. In describing them we must adopt some order that the matter may be intelligible; but in practice they can be all intermingled in any way in which they spring from the soul. Remember the end and object of the whole exercise is to converse with God; if you are doing this therefore you are doing well. I have said that there should always be some short meditation, because I am speaking to beginners of whom this is true; but for those more advanced this become less necessary, and after a time might be only a distraction.

If the mind is all day long full of worldly and distracting thoughts and imaginations suggested by business, amusements, conversations, study, light reading, etc., it is evidently necessary to think of some holy subject in order to be able to pray with any fervor or recollection.

When, on the other hand, a person leads a quiet, secluded life, with few distractions, regular spiritual readings and frequent reflections on spiritual subjects, the soul is very easily moved to pray, and less meditation is necessary. After a time, with holy and contemplative souls, any train of thought would become a distraction; they are at once, and without effort, absorbed in God. We may liken them to gunpowder; the slightest thought of God acts like a spark and sets them at once in a blaze, whereas distracted souls are like damp wood that requires much artificial help to kindle it into a flame.

3. "How long ought mental prayer to last?"

No general rule can be laid down. The real answer is that if we only consider the matter in itself, the longer mental prayer can last the better for the soul; but taking into account the weakness of most souls, and the many occupations that cannot be neglected, half-an-hour in the day is a reasonable average time. If however half-an-hour appears too long, begin with fifteen minutes. One little quarter of an hour in each day is surely not too long to devote to the grandest of all occupations – conversation with God Himself. People who are less constantly occupied and more devout could easily spend two half hours: one in the morning, one in the evening, in this holy exercise. The appetite for this spiritual manna will increase by satisfying it. The more you allow yourself, the more you will want. This may be said in conclusion; that the longer time you spend in fervent and humble mental prayer the more rapid will be your progress in the way of virtue.

4. "When is the best time for mental prayer?"

Most certainly early in the morning. If it be faithfully performed in the early morning, this spiritual banquet is secured, but when once the duties of the day have begun, it is far more difficult to find time. Moreover, the early morning is the quietest time, and is far less liable to interruption. The brain, being then refreshed with sleep, is more able to attend to prayer. Besides all this. God seems more inclined to give His graces to those who mortify their sloth and arise early in order to praise Him; and all those who practice mental prayer will agree that the early morning is the best time to converse with God. This seems to be the lesson conveyed by the act of the manna being rained down in the desert early in the morning and melting with the first rays of the sun, "that it might be known to all, that we ought to prevent the sun to bless Thee, and to adore Thee, at the dawning of the light."[102]

5. "I have no time for mental prayer."

It is difficult to answer this common objection with a grave face. What it means is, "I do not want to take the trouble to make mental prayer." To say that would be at least honest. But to plead the want of time to spend 15 minutes out of the 24 hours in

---

[102] Wisdom xvi, 28

conversation with God is childish. What would the same persons say if they saw a way of gaining £5 or even 5 dollars employing one quarter of an hour in a particular pursuit well within their power? How quickly would time be found! Who is there that does not spend a quarter of an hour daily in useless conversation or idle reading or in doing nothing? I should reply, make time by arising a quarter of an hour earlier. All that is required is a little more earnestness in the one all-important business of salvation.

6. *"Where should mental prayer be made?"*

God is everywhere, and there is no place in which we cannot find Him, but in order to speak to Him reverently and without distraction, a private place should be sought. "Thou when thou shalt pray, enter into thy chamber, and having shut the door, pray to thy Father in secret."[103] Our Lord prescribed this secrecy to avoid ostentation and vain-glory, but another motive would be to shun distraction. But for those who have no suitable place at home, the church is always ready.

7. *"What book shall I use?"*

For those who are able to think a little for themselves, a text of Holy Scripture is the best food

---

[103] St. Matt. vi. 6.

for meditation, or a sentence from the Following of Christ. But many need their thinking to be done for them by another, and this very thing often causes a difficulty. They come across a book which furnishes them with the thoughts and reflections of a man who probably was in a completely different state, both mental and spiritual, from their own. His thoughts most excellent and fruitful for himself, are not suited to them, to their difficulties, their temptations, their duties. The consequence is that they find these thoughts "dry" – that is, they do not come home to those using the book with any force or light, although so good in themselves. As a general rule the simpler a book is, the better for practical use, and each one should try to find an author, or to select some parts out of a book, suited to the needs of his own soul. If you come across one thought that strikes the mind, immediately delay upon it, as a bee on a honey flower, and strive to draw from that one thought your acts, petitions and resolutions. If the thought suggested by the book enables you thus to pray and to resolve, it has done its office; and you need by no means distress yourself even if the acts elicited and the resolution formed do not seem to have any evident and immediate connection with the previous thought.

There is one snare, as has been said above, most carefully to be avoided – that is, to stop praying in order to refer to the book for more points of reflection; for this would be to give up intercourse with God in order to entertain new thoughts. On the other hand, it is well to have some other thought in store, in case you can pray no longer, and need some fresh light from the understanding to give impetus to the will. If you persist in using some book that does not suit your needs and fall in with your spiritual state, you will run the risk of suffering from a kind of mental indigestion, from trying to assimilate thoughts of another mind not fitted to be the food of your soul. The result will very probably be that you will abandon mental prayer in disgust, saying, "It's no use, I cannot meditate!" This would be as unreasonable as to give up eating because one particular kind of food disagreed with you, and you could not digest it. Find the food that will.

Simple thoughts on the four great truths of religion, on the Passion of Our Lord, or the mystery of the Blessed Sacrament, will suit the greater number of souls; and half the difficulty vanishes when it is clearly understood that one simple thought is amply sufficient as long as it helps you to pray, which is the real object of the exercise. Nor is it by any means necessary always to vary the thought, for often the same reflection repeated morning after morning, will suffice to help you to pray, and if so why change it! We eat bread day after day, and if one thought nourishes the soul morning after morning why change it for another? If it begins to pall and to produce distraction, then seek for another. One holy soul found matter for prayer and union with God for months together from the two simple words "Our Father." If they were sufficient to form matter for prayer for years together, why change? Yet some people would have been inclined to pull St. Francis by the habit and to say – "You have been saying 'My God and my all' for an hour now: had not you better go to the second point?"

8. "I am distracted."

Examine the causes of these distractions. If they arise from too great dissipation of mind during daily life, try to live more in God's presence. If from not having prepared any definite thought to dwell upon, the remedy is to have one always prepared. If from mere weakness of mind, do not be disturbed, use no violent effort but quietly turn the mind back to God. One thing at least to utterly avoid is to abandon mental prayer because you are distracted. By this you will please no one except the devil. He does all he can to make you give up mental prayer, because he knows full well that if you persevere in it you will be saved. If by causing you troublesome distractions he can make you abandon mental prayer, he has succeeded in his object. St. Francis of Sales tells us that if in mental prayer we are able to do nothing but continually banish distractions and temptations, we shall derive great profit from the exercise and please God. What more could be desired?

Lastly, to encourage souls to persevere in the sanctifying habit of mental prayer, it is well to remember that Benedict XIV granted an indulgence of seven years to those who make half-an-hour's mental prayer during the day, and a plenary indulgence if it is made once a month, on the condition of confession and communion, with prayers for the Pope's intention. Those who are members of the Holy Rosary Confraternity can also gain a hundred days' indulgence every time they make a quarter of an hour's mental prayer, and seven years with seven quarantines for every half-hour devoted to this holy exercise.

Printed in Great Britain
by Amazon